Read for a Better World™

BARYONYX

A First Look

TOM JACKSON

Lerner Publications ◆ Minneapolis

Educator Toolbox

Reading books is a great way for kids to express what they're interested in. Before reading this title, ask the reader these questions:

What do you think this book is about? Look at the cover for clues.

What do you already know about this dinosaur?

What do you want to learn about this dinosaur?

Let's Read Together

Encourage the reader to use the pictures to understand the text.

Point out when the reader successfully sounds out a word.

Praise the reader for recognizing sight words such as *had* and *it*.

TABLE OF CONTENTS

Baryonyx

Baryonyx was a dinosaur.
It lived one hundred and
twenty-five million years ago.

Baryonyx
bah-REE-on-icks

The dinosaur had a big mouth with sharp teeth. It looked like an alligator.

The dinosaur walked on two legs. It had a long tail.

It had large claws
on its fingers.

How could claws be useful?

The dinosaur was thirty feet (9 m) long.

It was as heavy
as a car.

The dinosaur lived by rivers. It walked in the water.

What other animals live in a river?

The dinosaur ate fish.
It grabbed them with
its claws.

What other animals eat fish?

The dinosaur is
not alive today.
But people
find its bones.

The bones teach us about how this dinosaur lived.

You Connect!

What is something you like about this dinosaur?

What else is as big as this dinosaur?

What other dinosaurs do you know about?

STEM Snapshot

Encourage students to think and ask questions like scientists. Ask the reader:

What is something you learned about this dinosaur?

What is something you noticed in the pictures of the dinosaur?

What is something you still don't know about this dinosaur?

Photo Glossary

alligator

bones

claws

teeth

Learn More

Greve, Meg, *Super-Incredible Dinosaurs*. Mankato, MN: Black Rabbit Books, 2025.

Hulick, Kathryn. *Dinosaurs*. Minneapolis: Abdo Reference, 2023.

Spiro, Ruth. *Baby Loves Paleontology*. Watertown, MA: Charlesbridge, 2024.

Index

Photo Acknowledgments

The images in this book are used with the permission of: © Daniel Eskridge/Shutterstock Images, pp. 5, 10-11, 13, 18, 23 (claws); © Mariavspetrova/Dreamstime.com, pp. 6, 23 (teeth); © Ernie Hounshell/Shutterstock Images, pp. 7, 23 (alligator); © Aleks49/Shutterstock Images, p. 9; © Savoul Pelister/Shutterstock Images, p. 12; © Dotted Yeti/ Shutterstock Images, pp. 14-15; © Andrey Atuchin/Wikimedia Commons, pp. 14-15; © YuRi Photolife/ Shutterstock Images, p. 16; © Ingrid Pakats/Shutterstock Images, p. 17; © Wikimedia Commons, pp. 20, 23 (bones).

Cover Photograph: © Daniel Eskridge/Shutterstock Images

Design Elements: © Mighty Media, Inc.

Lerner Publications Company
An imprint of Lerner Publishing Group, Inc.
241 First Avenue North
Minneapolis, MN 55401 USA

For reading levels and more information, look up this title at www.lernerbooks.com.

Main body text set in Mikado a Medium. Typeface provided by Hannes von Doehren.

Library of Congress Cataloging-in-Publication Data

Names: Jackson, Tom, 1972-author
Title: Baryonyx : a first look / Tom Jackson.
Description: Minneapolis : Lerner Publications, [2026] | Series: Read about dinosaurs | Includes bibliographical references and index. | Audience: Ages 5-8 | Audience: Grades K-1 | Summary: "Young readers will love learning about Baryonyx, a dinosaur that looked like an alligator and was as tall as a giraffe. Photorealistic images help bring this dinosaur to life"—Provided by publisher.
Identifiers: LCCN 2025013671 (print) | LCCN 2025013672 (ebook) | ISBN 9798765689820 library binding | ISBN 9798348029081 paperback | ISBN 9798765697740 epub
Subjects: LCSH: Baryonyx—Juvenile literature
Classification: LCC QE862.S3 J3283 2026 (print) | LCC QE862.S3 (ebook) | DDC 567.912—dc23/eng/20250721

LC record available at https://lccn.loc.gov/2025013671
LC ebook record available at https://lccn.loc.gov/2025013672

Manufactured in the United States of America
1 - CG - 12/15/25